The Coconut Flan

The Coconut Flan

Written by María Isabel Tierra
Illustrated by Vivi Escrivá

HOUGHTON MIFFLIN   BOSTON • MORRIS PLAINS, NJ

California • Colorado • Georgia • Illinois • New Jersey • Texas

Houghton Mifflin Edition, 2001

Printed in the U.S.A.

ISBN: 0-618-09384-2

6789-FL-06 05 04

4

Today there is a party at Tía Chabela's.

All my cousins are in the kitchen, helping my aunt.

Tía Chabela says, "And now, let's make some coconut flan. Oh, I forgot to buy coconut!"

Tía Chabela gives me money. She says, "Ligia, go to the store and get some shredded coconut."

I sing on my way to the store, "Shredded coconut. Shredded coconut. Just a bit of shredded coconut."

Just then I see a cat drinking some milk.

I get to the store and ask, "May I have some milk, please?"

I return to Tía Chabela's. She says, "But Ligia, I already have milk. I need shredded coconut. Please go back to the store."

I sing on my way to the store, "Shredded coconut. Shredded coconut. Just a bit of shredded coconut."

Just then I see a neighbor putting sugar in her coffee.

I get to the store and ask, "May I have some sugar, please?"

I return to Tía Chabela's. She says, "But Ligia, I already have sugar. I need shredded coconut. Please go back to the store."

I sing on my way to the store, "Shredded coconut. Shredded coconut. Just a bit of shredded coconut."

Just then I see a hen laying some eggs.

I get to the store and ask, "May I have some eggs, please?"

I return to the house. Tía Chabela says, "But Ligia, I already have enough eggs, milk, and sugar for two flans! But I still don't have shredded coconut!"

I say, "Let's make two coconut flans without coconut!"

And we made so much flan that my cousins and I had a great time.